BL
South Carolina
HARBOR ISLAND
HARBOR RIVER
HUNTING ISLAND
FRIPP ISLAND
N
W
E
S
North Carolina
South Carolina
Georgia
Atlantic Ocean
Florida
0 50 100 200
Nautical Miles

Enjoy your fishing
even in the Rain!

Pamela Porter

Published 2022 by Pamela S Porter
Print by Signature Book Printing
https://signature-book.com

All Illustrations and Art Design:
Tamara Isaak-Harrington

Web Design: David Robinson

Fishing in the Rain is a true story.

ISBN: 978-0-578-26138-6

http://fishingintherain.net

DEDICATION

Dedicated to my husband Jim, may our love for each other, adventure and the great outdoors continue to grow as we enjoy this beautiful life together.

To our grandson Jake, your passion for fishing and quality family time in the low country was the inspiration for this book. May you always remind us to not let a little rain stop us from enjoying what we love in life!

ACKNOWLEDGMENTS

Raining Cats and Dogs

- **Jim Porter, Husband**
  - Addy, Small Munsterlander
- **Jake, Grandson**
  - Lola, Maltipoo
  - Roxie, Teacup Yorkie
- **Elizabeth Cavanaugh, Daughter**
  - Moxie, English Setter
  - Josie, Kerry Blue
  - Jax, Bengal
- **Seth Porter, Son**
  - Cloe, French Bulldog
  - Timber, Australian Cattle Dog
- **Scott Franssen, Brother**
  - Zoe, Goldendoodle
- **Pat Franssen, Brother**
  - Tucker, Norwich Terrier
  - Maggie Grace, Norwich Terrier
- **Tamara Isaak-Harrington, Illustrator**
  - Rufus, Hound/Beagle
  - Hugo, Mixed Breed
- **Jody Hayward, Port Royal Sound Foundation**
  - Indi, Golden Retriever
- **Amber Larck, Conservation Bank**
  - Olly, Mixed Breed
  - Remi, German Shepherd/Lab
- **Emily Oakman, Forestry Association**
  - Bruce, Corgi
  - Freya, Great Pyrenees
- **Kaylynn Caldwell, Friend**
  - Koko, Siamese
  - Suki, Siamese
- **David Shedlarz, Friend**
  - Lilly P, English Bulldog
  - Jean Pierre, French Bulldog
  - Gracie, English Bulldog
  - Maxwell, English Bulldog
- **Barb Sommers, Friend**
  - Maggie, Brittany
  - Jack, Tabby
- **Mimi Elder, Friend**
  - Sophie, Russian Blue
- **Candy Spadafora, Friend**
  - Ruffles, American Longhair

Caleb, with son Jake, 9 flew from Columbus OH. Caleb is head coach for Columbus Crew Major League Soccer team. 2020 MLS Champions!

Caleb played professional soccer before coaching. Jake and his brother Colin both play soccer. Sister Stella dances ballet. Mom, Andrea also played soccer in college. Athletic family!

3

Caleb and Jake came into the Low Country thursday night, October 2019. Daddy Jim chartered with Papa Bear for a fishing trip to ensure a successful day!

Jim, Caleb and Jake were going fishing. But they woke to blustery weather. Raining cats and dogs! The captain called to cancel their fishing trip. It was not safe.

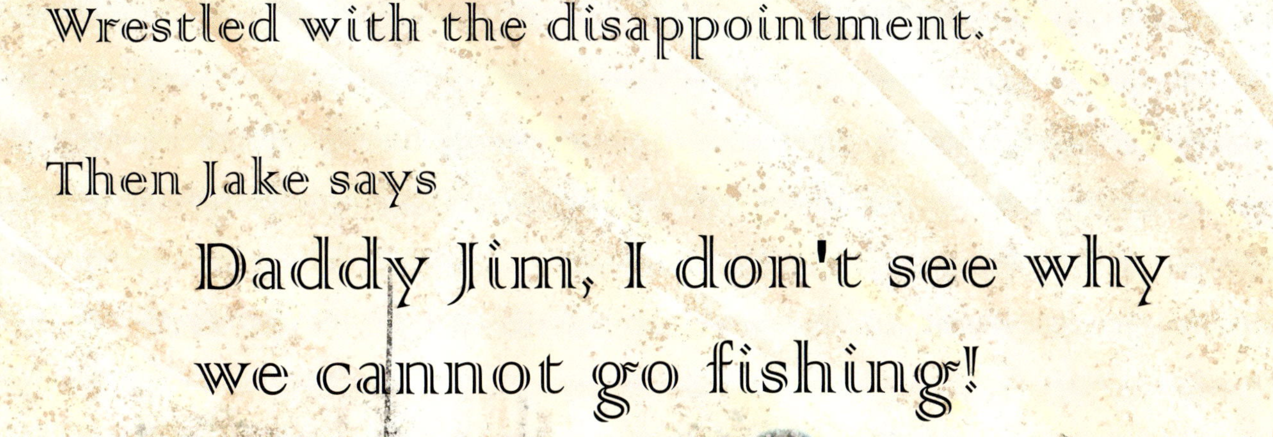

Jake was devastated! He pondered the situation. Wrestled with the disappointment.

Then Jake says

Daddy Jim, I don't see why we cannot go fishing!

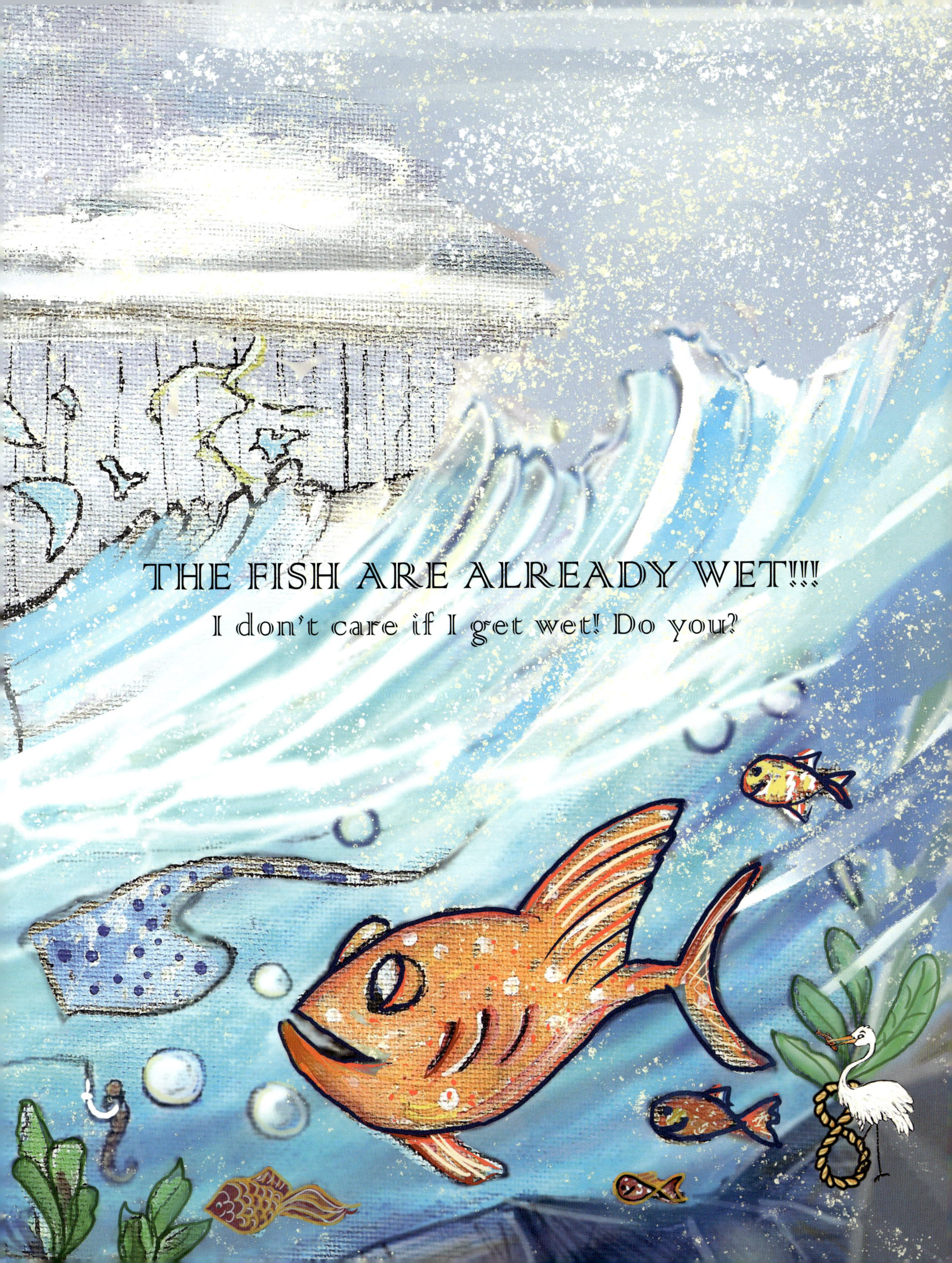

THE FISH ARE ALREADY WET!!!

I don't care if I get wet! Do you?

9

You are right!

OK, let's buy fishing rods and bait. If we are going fishing in the rain, we need good equipment and fresh bait!

They jump into the truck and go to Southern Drawl Outfitters.

Southern Drawl Outfitters

Jake picks out a fishing rod and reel. Josh, from the fish shop rigs the rods and gives Daddy Jim and Jake the bait; minnows, shrimp and squid.

Now to gear up with foul weather gear. Daddy Jim put his on and used Grandmother Pam's for Jake to wear. Which was too big for him but he did not care, he was going fishing!!!

They took their gear and headed to the dock in the pouring rain!

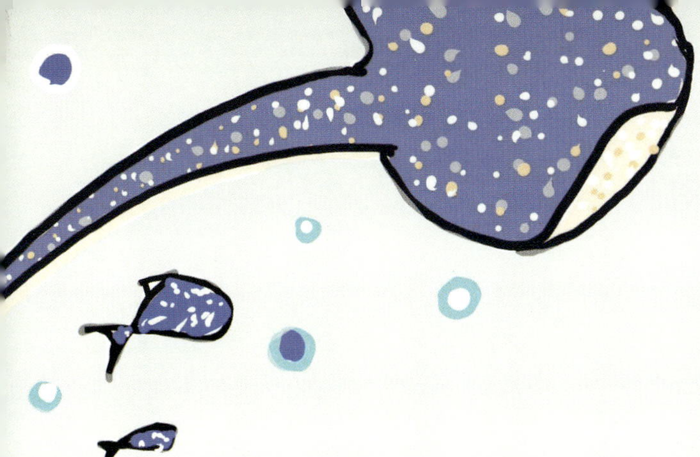

The first rod was baited and thrown into the water at 10:30 am. In ten minutes Jake caught his first fish! A beautiful speckled sea trout 16" long, about 2 pounds. A keeper!

Next catch was a stingray! They are fighters. But once up it's a big surprise! It has long gills and little mouth and a long tail with a barb on it. And you do not want to get caught by that barb!

Next, a shark! About two feet long. Fought hard. All muscle and incredible swimmer. Jake brought up the shark.

WOW!

Now What! How to get a Shark off the Hook!

Sharks

More speckled sea trout, 15" and 16". Beautiful fish with a lot of coloration.

The rain began to slow, Daddy Jim and Jake decided to take the 18' fishing boat across the Colleton River to a narrow estuary next to Spring Island.

They loaded up the boat with tackle and rods and cruised across the waters.

They eased to a tranquil spot and anchored. Daddy Jim gave Jake a rod baited with shrimp. Within 10 minutes Jake got his first strike! He brought in a crab. Then a bit later a nice red fish!

Red fish are unique because you keep the smaller ones, 15-23". The larger ones, are not legal to keep because they spawn and make new baby red fish.

The rain came again
in buckets! Raining cats
and dogs!

They pulled up the anchor and cruised back home fast in a complete down pour!

The waters were choppy, but Daddy Jim piloted the boat safely to the dock.

They shake off for a minute under the roof of the dock. Should they go in and get something to eat?

Jake said, No let's keep fishing. Daddy Jim was amazed, but he said, absolutely, the Fish are Already Wet!!!

The next fish was the biggest of the day! Jake had a rod baited with shrimp. The rod went wham, it doubled over in half! Jake held on and started reeling. The fish kept pulling.

BIG FISH!

Jake would reel, Daddy Jim would reel.
Jake would reel, Daddy Jim would reel.
Jake would reel, Daddy Jim would reel.
Jake would reel, Daddy Jim would reel.

Daddy Jim carefully helped by using a net. He netted the big red fish!

What a smile on Jake's face. Each fish is exciting, but this one was the biggest of the day!

Jake took the fish and cradled it in his arms. The incredible emotion of success of this young boy fishing with his grandfather.

The picture was posted on FaceBook, and tagged the phrase

Catch, Hug and Release.

4:30 pm. Stop!

They were exhausted!

Daddy Jim cleaned the fish. Jake watched.

They cooked their first fish for breakfast the next morning.

It was DELICIOUS!
Success! They had a ball!

Began at 10:30 am and finished at 4:30 pm without breaks, no food or water.

Just FISH, FISH, FISH!

A total of 13 fish.

Fishing in the Rain, Why Not? The Fish are already Wet!

Incredible perseverance and tenacity of fishing in the rain!

FISHING for the next Story
36